IN PLACE OF A CAMERA

MICHAEL WISE

Childhood Reminiscences of
World War II

*To Vicky.
With love,
Dan (Michael Wise's sister).
Thanks for so much help.*

Reproduction of original watercolours and printing by Omicron Reprographics
01227 768275
www.omicronrepro.co.uk

FOREWORD

As a twelve year old boy, out of the uncountable air battles I witnessed during the Battle of Britain, one in particular sticks out in my mind. Two of the aircrew from a shot-down bomber came swinging down to earth by parachute, so near that it looked as if they were going to land only a few houses away. Two things caught my eye. The first was that one of the parachutes was orange as opposed to the usual white; the second was that accompanying the parachuting airmen was a wheel, spinning down to earth from the bomber.

In later years I thought, 'If only I had had a camera at the time to record that scene so I could share it with my children and grandchildren'. I had a simple Kodak box camera, but like most things in the war, film was in short supply due to it being wanted for military purposes.

So as an amateur artist I did the next best thing to a photo – I painted the parachute scene. Having done that it resulted in other scenes I would like to share and record for future generations, which culminated in this collection of wartime recollections painted *in place of a camera*.

The illustrations depict scenes of where I was living at the time, not where I am now living. Several of the depictions will be seen as similar to their own by those who were children or youths during the war, particularly by those who lived in south east England.

The illustrations featured on BBC television after being displayed in an exhibition, on WWII, in a local museum.

Michael Wise

Canterbury

EXPERIENCING THE BLACKOUT

1938. My mother, sister and I walked to the town centre to experience the eerie, still atmosphere of a trial 'Blackout'. No street lighting was allowed, nor lighting in shop windows. Blackout blinds had to be used in houses to hide indoor lighting, so that if war was declared a conglomeration of lights (denoting a built-up area) could not be seen from the air as a navigational aid to German bombers. People were encouraged to wear white arm bands so they could be seen more easily; if wearing a white shirt, youths and young men displayed their shirt tails. Air Raid Precaution wardens patrolled the streets to ensure blackout regulations were being adhered to.

'Draw your curtains closer together!'

THE FIRST AIR RAID WARNING

On 3rd September 1939, my friends and I were playing in the garden when my mother called me in to hear the 11.15am radio broadcast by the Prime Minister, Neville Chamberlain, telling the nation whether or not Germany had withdrawn its forces from invading Poland. It hadn't. Therefore, the Prime Minister solemnly announced that war had been declared on Germany. I rushed out to tell my friends. Within minutes the wails of the air raid sirens were heard: if the newsreels were to be believed, German bombers would appear immediately. One of my friends vaulted a fence leading to her garden. My other friends fled home like frightened rabbits, as did we all, wanting to be in our homes when the bombs fell. The long friendly sound of the 'all clear' followed shortly after. There was a suspicion that it was all a government exercise.

GAS MASKS AT THE READY

When I ran from the garden in a panic, four gas masks were lined up on the dining room table; my father's, my mother's, my sister's and mine. I put on the first gas mask which came to hand; it was father's. Had there been a gas attack, the gas would have seeped in because the mask was too large. As it happened, gas as a weapon was never used. It was thought inevitable that it would be because it had been such a horrific, formidable weapon in the previous World War. It had also been used by the Japanese against the Chinese, and by the Italians against the Abyssinians in their respective wars, which occurred shortly before WWII.

PROTECTING IMPORTANT BUILDINGS

After the declaration of war there was a predominance of soldiers. Their manpower was used for other things besides soldiering, as seen here where they are employed filling bags with sand, and stacking them against the wall of a cottage hospital to protect the building against blast. We delighted in the rare opportunity to work alongside soldiers by holding the bags open for them to shovel in the sand.

IDENTIFICATION CARD CHECK

Public transport was often boarded by soldiers or the police to check that passengers had a National Registration Identity Card. These were issued to every man, woman and child a month after war was declared. People had to carry the card by law; if they had children, theirs as well. Anyone who failed to produce a card was questioned and if they could not give a satisfactory answer they were taken off the bus or train and detained. People could be stopped anywhere by police or those in uniform, and asked to produce their card.

FIRST THINGS FIRST – DIGGING AN AIR RAID SHELTER

When I decided to spoil a large part of the garden by digging a hole to create an air raid shelter, to my surprise there was no objection from my parents. Together with my friends we took pleasure in making the hole as big and deep as we liked. The steel corrugated Anderson shelters had not yet been distributed to every householder, so in the meantime a hole had to serve the purpose. My parents had managed to obtain stout wooden planks to lay across as a roof, on top of which we piled the earth we had dug out. I made a crude wooden entrance, steps to go down and two long benches were installed for seating. The shelter was used every day during the ferocity of the Battle of Britain.

FIRST EXPERIENCE OF MAJOR AIR ACTIVITY

My sister and I, with a friend, were staying with my grandparents in a village on the Hampshire-Surrey border. When returning from a walk, low flying Dornier bombers swept overhead on their 'run-in' to drop bombs on the barracks at Aldershot. The job done, within minutes the bombers swept over us again on return to their base in France.

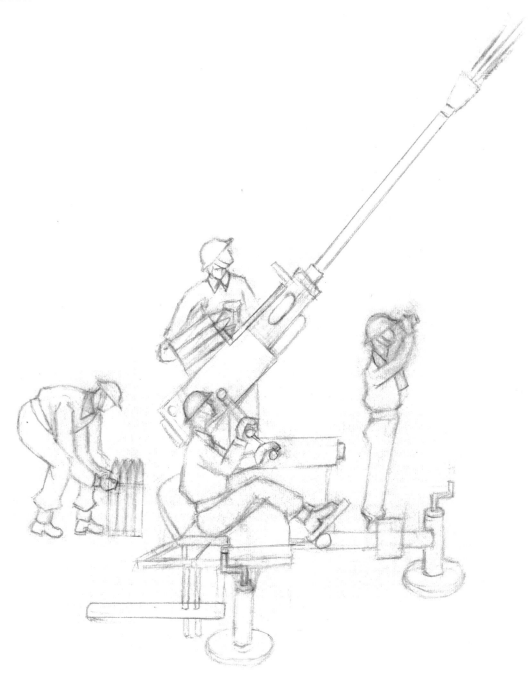

'CONQUER WE MUST, AS CONQUER WE SHALL'

10th May, 1940. Whilst having my hair cut by 'Benny the Barber' I heard those waiting to go in the chair say that Churchill had become Prime Minister in place of the appeaser Neville Chamberlain. Having been brought up to believe that the far-seeing Churchill (who had warned since Hitler came to power in 1933 that Germany was preparing for war) would be proved right, and needed one day to lead the nation against German militarism, I thought, 'Good now we are going to win the War!' His reassuring, inimitable voice over the airwaves telling the nation in his first broadcast as Prime Minister, 'Conquer we must, as conquer we shall' had every British citizen believing that too, even though we were losing the war on every front.

'We shall fight on the beaches, we shall fight on the landing grounds, we shall fight in the fields, and in the streets, we shall fight in the hills; we shall never surrender.'

INVASION EXPECTED THE NEXT DAY

When I came down to breakfast on 28th May 1940, my mother dramatically held before me a paper with the headlines 'Calais Falls'. Calais was poignant to me because shortly before the war, while on holiday at Ramsgate, we went on a day trip to Calais by paddle steamer. It brought home to me how very near France was. Now the might of the unstoppable German army was there! I could see no way how that invincible force could be stopped from crossing the 21 mile stretch of water. I cried myself to sleep that night feeling sure I would wake up to German soldiers marching through my town on their way to London. It didn't occur to me that before the Germans arrived I would have been woken up by an horrific bombardment which may well have resulted in our house being decimated by gun fire.

THE DUNKERQUE TRAIN

One of the procession of trains back from the defeat at Dunkerque halted at a nearby level crossing on an over-congested railway line, waiting for troop-laden trains in front to clear. The tired, dishevelled soldiers were on their way to a rehabilitation centre to be re-equipped to fight on. Here my sister and I have brought tea and buns from home, as did other onlookers, to refresh and feed the soldiers. They threw out items of clothing, equipment and firearms to convey the message that they were fed up with fighting, and fed up with war.

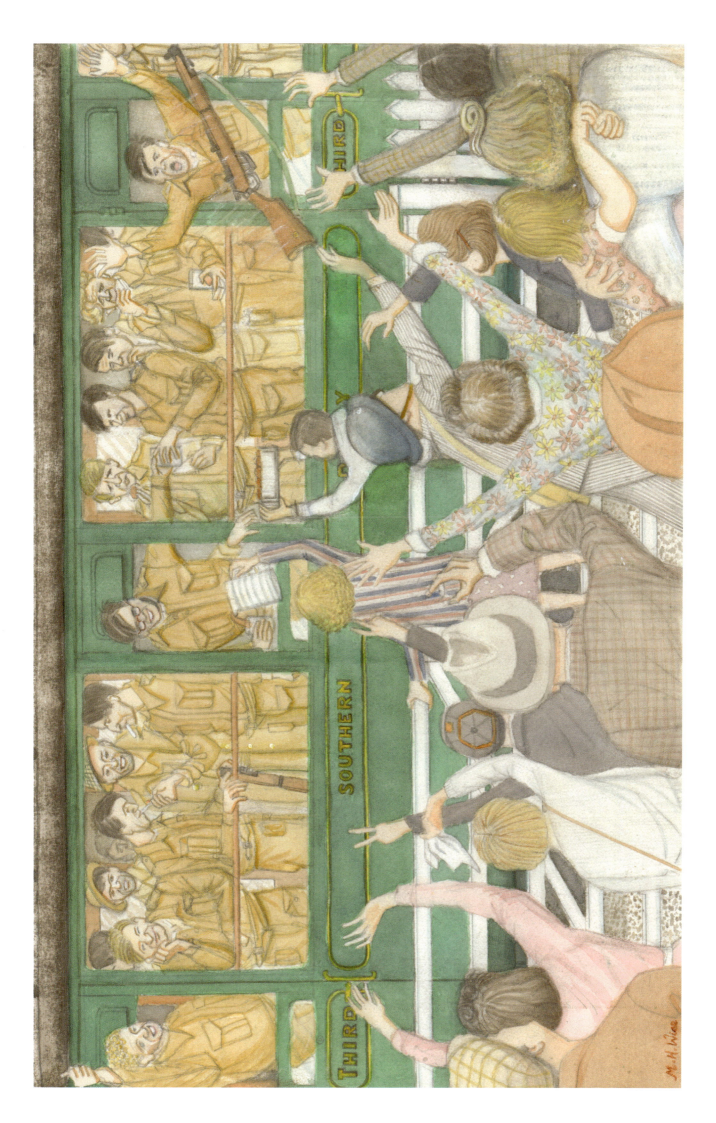

A STORY BOOK START

Little known to us, the sight of these low flying Spitfires, in what was known as 'vic' (vee) formation was to herald the Battle of Britain. At a time when we were losing the war, and the enemy was at the gate, it was a terrific morale booster to see this symbol of defiance. It gave the message that we weren't beaten yet, and weren't going to be! We waved frantically to these yet untried pilots. 'Well done boys' shouted a detective friend who was staying with us. During the next few months we were soon to learn the prowess of the Royal Air Force when it defeated the by far numerically superior German Air Force, and thereby put an invasion seriously in doubt.

'Never in the field of human conflict was so much owed by so many to so few'
– Winston Churchill to the House of Commons on the victory of the British fighter pilots over the German Air Force in the Battle of Britain.

THE GREAT AIR SHOW

During the Battle of Britain I woke up excitedly each morning thinking, 'What air show is the R.A.F. and the Luftwaffe (German Air Force) going to put on for me today?' Several of us gathered in the garden at 8am knowing that the show was about to commence with a backdrop of tangled vapour trails, and a sound track of whirling aircraft and machine gun fire as the German bombers made their way to London. No thought was given to the horrific suffering of the airmen whirling down to earth in their burning aircraft.

THE SPINNING WHEEL

Upon emerging from the air raid shelter after a ferocious air battle, we saw two German airmen sail down to earth accompanied by a spinning wheel from their shot down bomber.

CRASH LANDED SPITFIRE

This Spitfire had crash landed, probably due to a shortage of fuel. The irresponsible guards allowed us to climb in and out of it although the eight machine guns mounted in the wings were fully loaded. In our schoolboy exuberance we could easily have pressed the firing button on the control column, endangering the life of anyone entering the field.

SHOT DOWN MESSERSCHMITT FIGHTER

I came across this brought down Messerschmitt 109 fighter when cycling along a country lane. I found out later it was one shot down by Squadron Leader Tom Greave on 30th August 1940. It was piloted by Oberleutnant Axhelm of Jadgeschwader 27, stationed in northern France and who was taken prisoner. In the Battle of Britain the south east counties were littered with crashed aircraft.

TAKING COVER

Whilst playing in the fields it was frequently necessary to take cover under trees during fierce air battles. No matter what tree we sheltered under, cartridges and links from the machine gun belts tinkled through the branches from the fighting aircraft overhead. The fall-out was such a common occurrence that we never thought of saving the cartridges and parts of the machine gun belts. Had we done so they would have been valuable souvenirs today.

A MYSTERY FIND

I had wandered off from my friends when playing in a field, and found a hole covered with mounted sheets of corrugated iron. To my surprise beneath the sheets were the remnants of a Messerschmitt fighter. How it got there I do not know! I didn't tell my friends about the find because there was competition between us for who could collect the most souvenirs. I stopped taking pieces when I spied a 250lb bomb in the debris. I reported it to the police, but they didn't believe me, and so the bomb remained there. Among the pieces I took was a blue oxygen cylinder which I used as a hot water bottle.

A.R.P. HEADQUARTERS

This unassuming picture portrays a strong memory which sticks out in my mind because it depicts an incident when a Battle of Britain pilot had crash landed. A fulltime A.R.P. warden, upon reporting the whereabouts of the aircraft to A.R.P. Headquarters, had taken the pilot with him to the nearest phone. To the excitement of the control room staff the pilot, hot from battle, spoke to several of them. I was on standby as an A.R.P. messenger whose job it was to take messages to sector posts if telephone lines had broken down in an air raid. It earned me the Defence Medal, known as 'the spam' medal because it was as easy to obtain as buying a tin of spam, a popular tinned meat.

CYCLING AROUND

A few scenes when cycling around the countryside. After the Battle of Britain, invasion was still very much feared. Troops were employed to build machine gun posts, known as blockhouses; tank traps; and optimistically, compounds for captured German soldiers. *Optimistically* because if the invaders had got this far it would have been British troops who were taken prisoner, not the Germans. If the road led to a military installation, it was not unusual to see troops laying dynamite along the route.

INCENDIARY BOMBS

An irresponsible farmer allowed me and my friend to lever up incendiary bombs which, owing to a navigational error, had been dropped in his fields instead of the nearby town. We took them home, unscrewed the top under the fin, and emptied out the iron oxide. In this illustration, evacuees taken in by my parents, look on with their sons, and son's girlfriend, as they watch the flair-up of the oxide.

DICING WITH DEATH

Having seen what a spectacular 'firework' display the incendiary bombs gave, it prompted me and my friend to try and empty the inflammable cordite from the heaps of ammunition we collected from unguarded crashed aircraft. This, we imagined, would be another pyrotechnical source. Unlike the incendiary bombs, there was no screw on the cartridges to empty the content; the obstacle, therefore, was getting at the sealed cordite. So using our respective dining room tables as work benches, or a shed where there was a vice, we tried to pull off the bullet or canon shell at the head of the cartridge in order to try and get at the cordite. Another way was to hammer at the detonator at the base of the cartridge to make a hole for the cordite to come out of. We didn't realise it could have detonated the ammunition. Our parents, who were in another room, would have heard an explosion and come out to find a burning house or shed, and the mutilated remains of two dead sons.

THE TEAR GAS VAN

A.R.P. personnel used to arrive at schools regularly with a tear gas van; pupils entered it with an A.R.P. official to have their gas masks tested. The doors of the van were shut, the official would then discharge gas from a canister. I never encountered a failure of a gas mask, and I still don't know how such an emergency would have been dealt with in a gas-filled van if a mask had leaked.

LISTENING TO THE WIRELESS

The only way to obtain up to date news was by listening to the wireless, so it occupied a central part of life during the war. Television was about to come in, but its development had been stopped owing to television engineers being diverted to the far more important job of developing RADAR (a radio detection system which gave scans of enemy positions). Amusement was caused when Allied victories were announced on the news, and German broadcasters interrupted the announcements by blaring out, 'That is a lie!'. When the BBC found this was happening it was stopped by newsreaders going on to the next announcement without pausing, thus depriving the Germans of space to interject.

OUT OF THE BLUE

9th May 1941. I was in the garden when I heard the sound of aircraft. I looked up and saw two aeroplanes – a Messerschmitt chasing a much maligned Boulten-Paul Defiant fighter; *maligned* because the British fighter had no forward armament. Once the Germans realised this they found it was easy to shoot down, but the Defiant had a machine gun turret mounted behind the cockpit. Evidently the pilot of the Messerschmitt chasing the Defiant hadn't seen this. I saw a flash of machine gun fire coming from the rear of the British fighter. The pilot bailed out. I tore away on my bike in the direction he was descending and saw a column of people hurrying along a main road on the same quest, they turned off into a country lane. A crowd was surrounding a small commandeered lorry carrying the wounded pilot. He was taken to hospital where he died.

CRASHED HEINKEL 111

Onlookers are seen here viewing a Heinkel 111 bomber which had been forced to crash land when returning from a raid on London. As in the case of many crash landings, it was remarkable how pilots managed to halt their aircraft just short of crashing into trees. It was either good piloting or good luck – a bit of both I should imagine! The incident is recorded as having taken place on 11th May, 1941.

'THEY'VE GOT ORANGES AT TRICE'S'

It was amazing how soon long columns of people suddenly appeared on their way to a green grocer, when through the 'grapevine' it was heard that a supply of oranges, lemons or bananas had arrived at a shop. Such fruits had become almost extinct during the war owing to shipping space wanted for more important cargo.

NEAR DEATH EXPERIENCE

During the war many people escaped death owing to a fluke. This happened to me on the morning of 31st March, 1943 when I was about to cross a recreation ground as a short cut to the town. I got to the entrance when I realised I hadn't taken the shopping bag. Going back home to get it saved my life. When I arrived at the front gate the short steam blasts of an air raid siren meant an air attack was imminent. Bombs fell where I would have reached on my way to the town. The blast would have killed me. The top right hand picture of a soldier firing a Lewis gun was one of several gunners who claimed to have shot down one of the fighter-bombers. The small picture on the bottom right hand side shows me and my mother sheltering in a cupboard under the stairs when the bombs fell.

The central part of the illustration depicts the mangled body of Staffelkapitan Oberleutnant Paul Keller, who had led this devastating low level air attack on our town, known as a 'Tip and Run Raid' – so called because the fighter-bombers flew in at high speed, tipped their bombs, and then ran for home. The Secretary of the local branch of the British Legion happened to be passing by, and is seen here exposing the head of the shot down pilot.

THE FIRST EXPERIENCE OF A 'FLYING BOMB' (THE V-1)

Indoors we heard a fierce throbbing sound of an aircraft. We rushed outside and saw searchlights trained on a comparatively low flying, short winged aircraft. Anti-aircraft shells were bursting around it. It wasn't powered by a normal petrol engine but by a jet engine mounted on its tail. An American officer who was billeted on us by the name of Greg Maxwell, exclaimed, 'He sure is a brave pilot not to detour under that barrage!' We didn't realise there was no pilot. It was one of the first of many V-1 guided missiles to be trained on London which became known as a 'flying bomb', because that is what it was. It also had the nickname of 'doodlebug' on account of it becoming frighteningly stationary (doodling) in the sky before it dived to earth. If its giro was disturbed the bomb stopped before it got to London and fell on other towns in its path, which included the town where I was living.

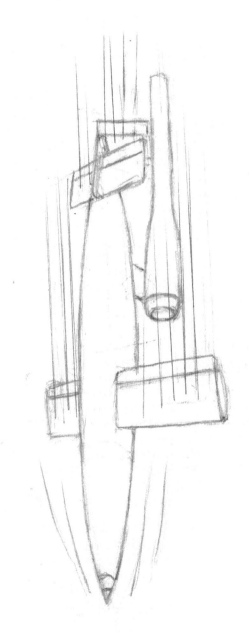

WOMEN LEFT AT HOME

One of the war time happenings which had the most impact on me was the low morality I encountered. The adage, 'When the cat is away the mice will play' has never been more exemplified than in the war. Permissiveness was endemic. Wives and sweethearts experienced loneliness when their fiancés or husbands were conscripted, particularly if they had been posted overseas and couldn't get home periodically. I was shocked to see women who I had respected, not hiding their illicit carryings-on.

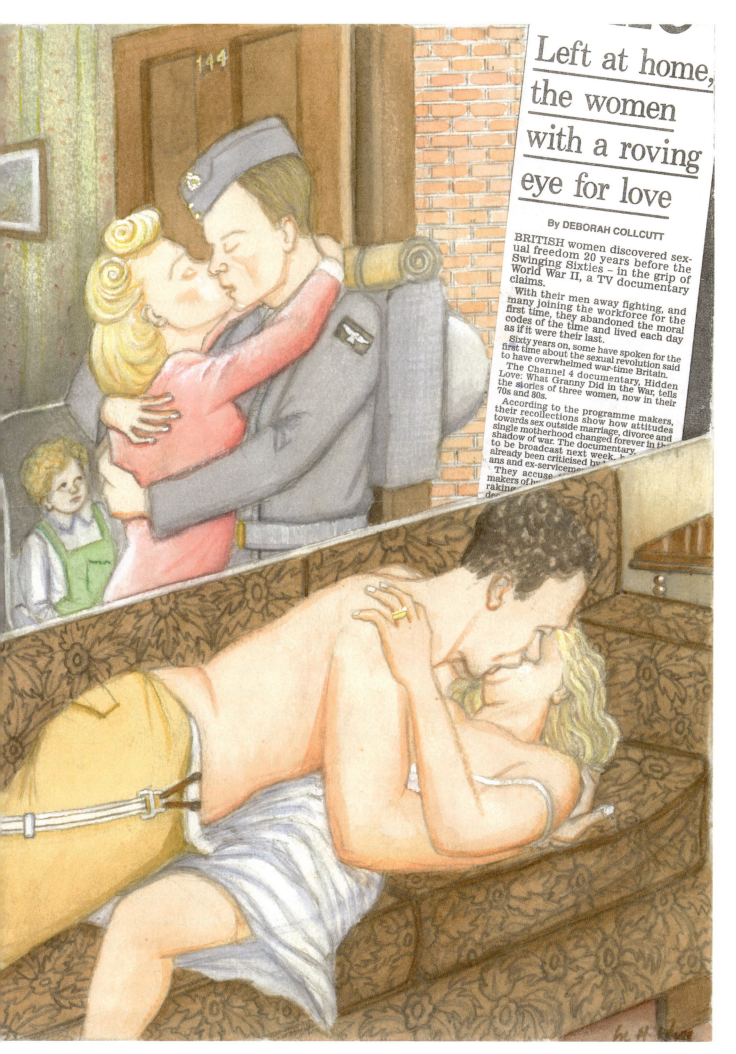

ADVANCED LANDING GROUNDS

As a weekend enjoyment my friends and I picked a good viewing point which looked down on fields compulsorily requisitioned from a farmer to serve as 'Advanced Landing Grounds' (temporary air fields). We delighted in seeing 'shot-up' American Thunderbolt fighters return from an operation, and watch the drama as they crash landed.

UNITED STATES ARMY AIR FORCE DUMP

We frequently went rummaging on a United States Army Air Force rubbish dump in a disused chalk pit. There was no class distinction among the scavengers: the better off and the less well-to-do rummaged side by side in their quest to find war time scarcities. What was considered rubbish to a G.I. (colloquial name for an American soldier) was something to be had, even thrown away packets of sweets. I am seen here taking away a dumped auxiliary fuel tank from a Thunderbolt fighter, which I used as a canoe.

'BUZZING' – ALL PART OF THE WAR

At the army stores depot where I worked as a civilian clerk, one or two of the girls had pilots as boyfriends. When returning from operations they would often fly a little above roof top height over the depot, circling the buildings several times (known as 'buzzing'). The girls were told by their boyfriends what they were going to do. As soon as low flying aircraft were heard, the girls raced out of the office, and waved frantically to the airmen. The airmen banked their aircraft so that the girls could see them in the cockpit. Such happenings were not considered out of place during the war.

OPERATION 'MARKET GARDEN'

We were in the garden when suddenly the sky was filled with Horsa Gliders being towed by Albermarle aircraft; they were on their way to an airport 28 miles away. From there the airborne force was flown to Arnhem in Holland to carry out 'Operation Market Garden.' Their objective was to capture a bridge over the Rhine to clear the way for our ground troops to invade that part of Germany. The airborne force was decimated due to a freshly trained German division being stationed in the Arnhem area. Unfortunately they found the plan of the attack on a captured British officer. Little did a neighbour of ours realise that among those flying overhead was one of their sons who was mortally wounded in the attack. He died three weeks later.

SAFE NOW FOR A VISIT TO LONDON

As the war drew to its end, and now that the bombing had stopped, people felt it safe to visit London. In celebration my mother took me with friends to see 'The Crazy Gang' at the Palladium. Before doing so we had tea at one of Lyon's renowned Corner House restaurants, famous among other things, for their smart black and white dressed waitresses, known as 'nippies' because of the way they nipped about when serving. With peace just around the corner the atmosphere was euphoric.

VICTORY IN EUROPE (VE DAY)

On 8th May, 1945 I was getting ready to go to work when the Prime Minister, Winston Churchill, announced on the wireless that Germany had surrendered. It was known as VE Day (Victory in Europe Day). A public holiday was declared and high streets soon became the centre of unbounded jollity. Respectful behaviour was thrown to the wind. The celebrations went on until the early hours of the morning. A few months later the euphoria was repeated when Japan surrendered, commemorated as VJ Day.

THINGS I WAS MOST PLEASED TO SEE GO……

- The ritual every night before going to bed of parting the curtains (against blackout regulations) to see if it was raining. If it was, it meant the visibility was too bad for German bombers to come over and I could go to sleep without fear. Weather forecasts were stopped on the wireless and in newspapers in order not to give the German Air Force information about weather conditions over the British Isles.

- Sweet rationing. Not having to go into a sweet shop and produce a ration book for confectionary; we were allowed three ounces a week. Rationing was not stopped immediately after the war, but towards the end it became lax.

- The removal of invasion obstructions from the beaches, and to be able to walk freely on them again.